MONKEYS AND APES WITHOUT TREES

MONKEYS AND APES WITHOUT TREES

Story and Photographs by Lilo Hess

Charles Scribner's Sons   **New York**

3

Over sixty million years ago some small, warm-blooded creatures, which suckled their young, started to live in trees. This gave them a better chance of survival than the animals that remained on the ground. These little animals were the tree shrews and their relatives. As time went by they perfected their way of living in trees. Their eyes moved forward so that they had a larger field of vision and could focus on an object with both eyes at the same time. Their hind limbs became strong, muscular legs, and their arms became longer. The hands developed so that they could grasp branches more securely and hold the food they ate in their hands. Since they could hop and climb with agility, they also could avoid their enemies better. Finally, their brain changed to coordinate these new abilities.

These animals were the early prosimians, which means "premonkeys" or "early monkeys" in Latin. Our present-day lemurs, tarsiers, pottos, lorises, and galagos are most like those early ancestors.

5

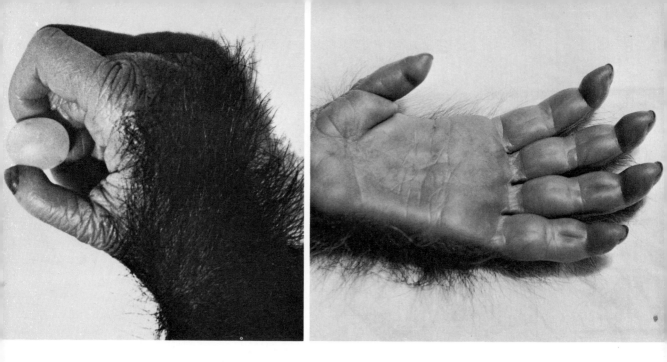

The development of nimble little hands was probably one of the most important changes in the early prosimians. It reached its perfection when the thumb became opposed to the fingers. Monkeys, apes, and man have the opposing thumb, which sets them apart from all the other animals. All monkeys and apes have five digits on each hand and foot, and most of them have flat nails like man. A few have slightly curved nails, and some of the prosimians have one or two claw-like nails which they use for grooming or scratching.

Prosimians are presumed to be the ancestors of all the primates. "Primate" means "first" or "top," and it is the highest form of life as we know it. It includes prosimians, monkeys, apes, and man.

In 1858 Charles R. Darwin stated that monkeys, apes, and man have common ancestors. This theory was attacked and disputed for years. The controversy came to a climax in 1925, when a schoolteacher named John T. Scopes in Dayton, Tennessee, was tried in court for teaching Darwin's theory. This was the famous "Monkey Trial," which was called "America's most amazing trial." Although Mr. Scopes was found guilty and fined one hundred dollars, the presiding judge said in his closing address: "A man who is big enough to search for the truth and find it, and declare it in the face of all opposition, is a big man." Today Darwin's theory has been accepted almost everywhere.

The only primate that has stopped living in trees permanently and always walks in an upright position is man. Early remains of human beings that have been found and pieced together show that man developed separately but branched from the same stem that produced all the other primates.

Scientists have divided the great varieties of primates into family groups, and not all are mentioned here.

Besides the before-mentioned prosimians, or half-monkeys, such as the lemurs, lorises, tarsiers, galagos, and pottos, there are the New World monkeys. These include the spider monkeys, woolly monkeys, capuchins, squirrel monkeys, and others. Most of these monkeys have a prehensile tail that can be used like a fifth "hand" to hold objects and to climb and swing with. All these monkeys live in South and Central America. Also from the New World are the tiny marmosets, which have been placed in a family group by themselves.

Old World monkeys include baboons, macaques, guenons, and many others. None of them have prehensile tails. They are sometimes called narrow-nosed monkeys in contrast to the broad-nosed monkeys of the New World. The largest nose in the monkey kingdom belongs to the proboscis monkey from Borneo.

The great apes are the most manlike primates, and none of them have tails. These are the gibbons, orang-utans, chimpanzees, and gorillas.

8

What makes monkeys and apes so fascinating to us is that they often remind us of someone we know, and we can see their superior intelligence in their behavior. All the smaller monkeys are less intelligent than the larger monkeys or the great apes. Among the land animals, monkeys and apes probably have the best ability to reason.

In an experiment, a baby chick, a puppy, and a young monkey were placed behind a wire partition which had an opening at one end. On the other side of the wire partition food was placed—grain for the chick, a hot dog for the puppy, and a banana for the monkey. The chick just pecked and pushed at the wire and never seemed to associate the opening with a means to get to the other side. The puppy ran against the wire in its eagerness to get at the food, then just stood there and whimpered. After a few minutes it ran back and forth along

the wire, discovered the opening by chance, and went through it to eat its food. The young monkey acted very differently. After one unsuccessful try to reach the banana through the wire, he looked around, noticed the opening, and went straight through it to eat his reward. The monkey had just arrived from the wild, so it was not used to a similar situation. It simply could reason better than the chick or the puppy.

Many experiments have been conducted to explore the reasoning powers of apes and monkeys, and many are still being done. In one test a seven-year-old chimpanzee was confronted with bananas hanging from the ceiling far out of his reach. He immediately took one empty crate from among several that were standing nearby and placed it directly under the bananas. When he saw that one crate was not high enough, he quickly piled two more crates on top of the first one, jumped up, and reached his prize.

Chimpanzees have been given pegboards and blocks to match up or to assemble in order to test their ability to recognize form, color, and differences in size. As soon as he understood what he was expected to do, a three-year-old chimpanzee took just a few seconds to place pegs with different shapes into the right holes on a board.

People of all ages are fascinated by these interesting relatives of ours and have tried to domesticate them and keep them as pets. More than a hundred thousand monkeys are imported yearly for the pet trade. They can be bought in almost every pet store and mail-order house, and they are sold as souvenirs or given away as prizes in raffles. The new owner is usually delighted for a few days and then disenchanted and unhappy. He finds it impossible to live with torn pillows, broken furniture and china, chewed-up books and papers, and the mess that an animal that is not housebroken can make. He cannot get a baby-sitter for his pet and must give up almost all vacations and social functions to which the animal cannot be taken.

Moreover, monkeys are very unpredictable. A monkey can throw its arms around you and hug you in a very human way. This display of love and trust by a wild creature makes you feel warm and wanted. But that same monkey can throw its arms around you, hold you tight, and bite very hard just a few minutes later, without your knowing what you have done to displease it.

If a monkey or ape is confined in a cage it usually becomes

inert, melancholy, and morose. It also becomes prone to such sicknesses as cage paralysis and pneumonia. No one will take the unwanted pet, and the owner is forced either to have it put to sleep or to give it to a pet store to be resold or to a laboratory for experiments.

Before purchasing such an almost-human pet, think very carefully about all the problems that surely will come up. People who love monkeys can show this love by restraining their desire to buy one. If you own a monkey already, everything must be done to make its life bearable and to keep it healthy and content.

The monkey most often sold in stores and through the mail-order catalogs is the common squirrel monkey, sometimes called moss monkey. This pretty animal never gets larger than

fifteen inches in body length, with a tail of almost the same length. It is a very lively, fairly friendly animal. In nature, in the tropical forests of Central and South America, it lives in huge colonies of up to five hundred individuals. It is brightly colored. The body is usually yellow, sometimes reddish gray, and the chest is white. The top of the head, the nose, and the mouth, as well as the tip of the tail, are mostly black. The face is almost without fur and looks pinkish. It has dark, expressive eyes and a childlike expression. A single baby is born and cared for by the mother.

A squirrel monkey is usually sold complete with cage for about thirty-five to forty-five dollars. The cage is not adequate to house it for any length of time, though for sleeping quarters the cage will do if it is outfitted with a little shelf or a wooden bird-nesting box. However, the monkey has to be let out to play and exercise for the better part of the day. Like all monkeys, the squirrel monkey is inquisitive, and destructive if left unsupervised. If a spare room can be outfitted with branches, swings, shelves, and toys, the squirrel monkey, or any other small or medium-sized monkey, can be kept there quite well. The door of this room should be equipped with a secure lock and it should be made of wire or screen, so that the animal can see and hear the rest of the family and feel part of it. Since this little monkey needs lots of companionship and entertainment, it is best to keep two of them together or to give one alone another pet to play with and to love.

A tame squirrel monkey may also be allowed outdoors. If the home is well isolated so that the monkey won't bother neighbors or get onto a highway, it need not be tied. If the monkey is contented and well established it will never go far from its home and will come when called. It usually answers its owner with high chirps and trills. A less tame monkey, which must be restricted in its movements, can wear a small harness or belt

around its waist with a long string tied to a tree. Some monkeys are very clever and avoid getting entangled in the string; others must be closely watched.

In spite of the squirrel monkey's bright colors, it is perfectly camouflaged when it sits in a sun-dappled tree or stands in the tall grass of a meadow. It is fun to watch this little fellow catch his own grasshoppers and other insects outdoors. It is very quick and never misses its quarry. It even catches and eats bumblebees. First it slaps the bee down with the palm of its little hand, then it rolls the bee quickly on the ground, bites the head off, and then eats the body leisurely.

A squirrel monkey can be easily frightened by quick movements and shrill, loud voices. If it gets too excited it might bite. It should never be in drafts, and if it gets wet in the rain it should be dried immediately because it catches cold easily. It should be allowed to sunbathe as often as possible. Like all captive monkeys it should be fed multiple-vitamin supplements and cod-liver oil.

Squirrel monkeys seem to like meat and should get bits of lean hamburger and all kinds of insects as well as mealworms. When moths gather around an outdoor lamp during summer evenings, the squirrel monkey doesn't seem to mind being awakened and let out to catch some.

The most common foods for pet monkeys are oranges, grapes, apples, bananas, pears, sweet and white potatoes, lettuce, spinach, kale, carrots, sweet corn, celery, and all berries in season. Many also like an assortment of flowers, buds, and leaves. Larger monkeys can be given some dog food or horse meat. Milk is relished by most primates, and the vitamins can be fed in a bowl of milk. Some monkeys enjoy their vitamins directly from the dropper. Whole wheat and raisin breads, cereal, eggs, and the commercial monkey pellets should also be given. Variety is very important to stimulate their appetite. Each individual has different preferences, and the diet must be adjusted to each monkey's needs. The quantity depends on the size of the animal. For small monkeys the food must be cut into bite-size pieces, while the large ones can eat most fruits whole. If two or more monkeys eat together the food should be cut into pieces so that all can get a piece of each kind of fruit. Everything must be washed carefully so that insecticides are removed. The previous owner of the monkey or the store from which it was purchased should be consulted and the established diet followed, until one knows the habits of the animal well. Changes can be made after the animal has adjusted to its new life. Candy, greasy foods, chewing gum, tobacco, and alcoholic beverages should never be given to a primate. As a treat a little ice cream, raisins, unsweetened cookies, or dog yummies can be given.

Toys for all small monkeys should be things that can be taken apart, torn up, or manipulated—containers with lids in which a small object or stone has been placed, pine cones that can be pulled apart and the seed eaten, or a baby rattle, hard rubber toys, a hand mirror on a string, as well as wooden blocks or old spoons. Do not give all the toys at one time. The monkey soon will tire of one kind and can then be handed something different.

Much more difficult to keep than the squirrel monkey, but sold just as frequently, are the much larger woolly monkeys and spider monkeys. These monkeys are usually sold when they are very young. Since they are often sick, undernourished, frightened, and unhappy, they give the impression that they would be quiet, gentle, and undemanding house companions. The sale price varies from seventy-five to two hundred dollars. The cage that dealers usually recommend for these animals is completely inadequate to house them. After a few months it probably is even too small to serve as sleeping quarters.

A fully grown spider monkey may have a body length of twenty-five to thirty inches and a tail that is even longer. It has extremely long, "spidery" legs and arms. Its native home is in

the tropical forests ranging from Mexico to Bolivia and in southern Brazil. There are many subspecies and each species is of a different color or shade. A spider monkey might be reddish, gold, buff, black, brown, or even white.

The agility of spider monkeys in the trees is beautiful to see. They gracefully leap from tree to tree, swing on vines and branches with their long arms, and hang by their tails. When they stand or walk erect, they steady themselves with the tail. If these monkeys are kept without trees and deprived of their acrobatic activities, they lose much of their spirit and all of their grace and beauty.

The appealing woolly monkey looks like a chubby, pot-bellied version of the spider monkey. But its fur is dense and plushy while that of the spider monkey is long and silky. Woolly monkeys may be black, gray, or brown. Some have heads and limbs darker than the rest of their bodies. They have a melancholy expression, which perhaps may be one reason so many people can't resist taking one home. Most woolly monkeys are sold when they weigh about three or four pounds. At that size they can eat by themselves but need lots of care and affection. A fully grown woolly weighs about fifteen pounds and has a body from twenty-five to thirty inches long and a tail of about the same length.

Woollies come from the upper reaches of the Amazon River where they live in large, very vocal family groups. They live in trees but often descend to the ground to hunt insects or search

for flowers and berries. They carry their tails high when they walk and the tip is always curled or looped. The tail is very thick and muscular. It is covered with the same thick fur as the body, except for the underpart of the last six or eight inches, which is a naked pad, particularly adapted for grasping. A spider or woolly monkey can pick up a small grape or raisin with the tip of its remarkable tail.

The majority of imported woollies suffer from a disease which causes the bones to soften and for which there is no real cure as yet. When woolly monkeys have this disease they appear quiet, gentle, and listless, and sometimes their eyes look bulgy. Good food, vitamins, fresh air, exercise, and lots of sunshine sometimes keep this sickness in check.

Like all monkeys they should be kept out of drafts. A healthy woolly can stand fairly cold weather and even likes to play in snow for short periods, but it must have a heated place to get warm and dry afterwards.

Besides the regular monkey food, woollies are particularly fond of fresh leaves and blossoms. Naturally no insect spray should be on the plants they eat. Without trees to climb they are only a shadow of their happy active selves. If at all possible they should be let outdoors. They usually stay very close to their home, playing in the treetops, sunbathing, catching insects, and munching on plants. Many monkeys eat whole handsful of soil, which might give them needed minerals.

Though woolly monkeys have a reputation for being the

gentlest, most affectionate of all pet monkeys, a healthy adult woolly is not really trustworthy and can inflict serious wounds. It might get angered if its owner scolds another household pet or speaks harshly to someone and thereupon attack the nearest person, even its owner. It also shows immediate likes and dislikes of strangers, clothing, or gestures. It might even object to a handshake or an embrace between its owner and other members of the family or friends.

If possible, a woolly should be kept with a companion. Two woolly monkeys are not much more work than one, and the animals will be happier and healthier.

A cage for woollies should be outdoors if possible, and for colder climates it should have a heated indoor part as well. It should be at least eight feet wide, eight feet long, and ten feet high. It must be constructed of strong wire and must have a good lock that cannot be opened by the monkey. Branches, twigs, platforms, and ropes, as well as a sleeping-box placed high, should be in every cage that confines a primate, just as in the before-mentioned "spare room." The bottom of the cage should have either linoleum that can be easily cleaned or some absorbent material that can be brushed up, such as woodshavings or straw. It is almost impossible to housebreak a monkey, and reports of persons who claim that their pet uses the toilet are usually exaggerated. The only primates that can sometimes be toilet trained are young apes, with the exception of the gibbon, which is not known to become housebroken.

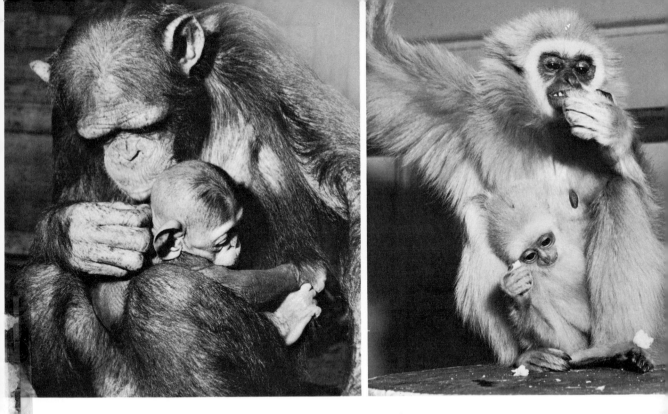

A monkey or ape mother carries her baby on her body wherever she goes. The youngster sometimes rides on her back and sometimes clings to her neck or chest when she walks about. When the mother sits down to feed, the baby that is a few months old will sample some of her food, but milk is its only real nourishment for quite a while. Smaller monkeys mature more quickly than the great apes. Apes might nurse their babies for over a year, while monkeys such as the woolly nurse for about six to eight months. The mother is almost constantly occupied with her child. She plays with it, scolds it if it does not behave, cleans and grooms it. Adult monkeys groom each other too. Grooming plays a vital part in the social life of monkeys and apes. The female grooms her mate, her children, and other females in the group. They in turn will groom her. People often think that fleas are what the monkeys or apes pick from their companion's fur and often eat, but it is specks of salt from the skin, loose flakes of skin, or other matter that might get into the animal's fur.

When a baby monkey or ape is captured in the wild and taken from its mother, it looks for comfort to its foster parent. Since one cannot carry such an infant about all the time, a substitute "mother" must be found. A turkish towel or other soft material or a cuddly stuffed toy is a good substitute. The baby can tow it along and clutch it when awake or during sleep.

Like any human baby, the infant ape or monkey needs a lot of rest and sleep. It will do little else but eat and sleep for the first few months of its life, and it should not be played with roughly or for too long. It should be fed every few hours. Standard human baby formulas are good for all monkeys and apes, or they can be given one part evaporated milk mixed with one part of water, a few drops of multiple vitamins, and a teaspoonful of Karo syrup to sweeten it, in a standard baby bottle. A nine- or ten-pound baby ape will drink six to eight ounces per feeding, and the three-pound monkey about half that amount. Most baby monkeys will stop when they have had enough and should not be forced to drink more than they want. If an animal won't eat at all for a day or two, the veterinarian should be consulted.

Most baby monkeys that are bought in stores have been weaned and can be given commercial baby foods such as meat and vegetables, cereals, and fruit juices. They usually are fond of mashed bananas. They can get milk mixed with some cereal right out of a cup or bowl.

Capuchin monkeys, or, as they are sometimes called, "ringtails" or "sapajous," are not sold as pets as frequently at the present time as they once were. These monkeys used to be the constant companions of organ grinders, who trained them to beg for pennies; and they also were used to perform in circuses or carnivals. They were often mistreated and badly cared for by owners who took advantage of their friendliness, great intelligence, and quick learning ability. Since their numbers in nature were greatly reduced through this constant demand, some restrictions have now been placed on their import.

There are many subspecies of the capuchin monkeys. All come from Central or South America, where they live in

troupes. They are quite vocal, chirping and chattering while they climb high in the treetops. Their tail is also prehensile, although not as much as that of the woolly or spider monkeys. When mature they can bite and are just as destructive and inquisitive as other monkeys. They need about the same food and care and the same type of cage as the woolly and spider monkeys, though the capuchins are somewhat hardier.

Because of their size, the marmosets, smallest of all the monkeys, are frequently sold in pet stores. Since they are so tiny, many people consider them ideal house pets, but they are quickly disillusioned. All marmosets are extremely delicate and need constant attention, veterinary care, and sacrifices from their owners.

Marmosets come from South America, where they live mostly in trees. There are about thirty different kinds, the smallest of them being the pygmy marmoset, which weighs only about four to five ounces when fully grown. Most marmosets are brightly colored, and some have pretty crests and tufts. They all have long tails which are not prehensile. They trill, chirp, and chatter as they leap and hurry through the branches. The one generally for sale in pet stores is the "common marmoset," which has white ear tufts on its little face. Its body is a mottled grayish brown. It is probably the most hardy marmoset and becomes quite tame if treated gently.

A female marmoset usually gives birth to twins, which the father carries on his back. At feeding time he transfers the

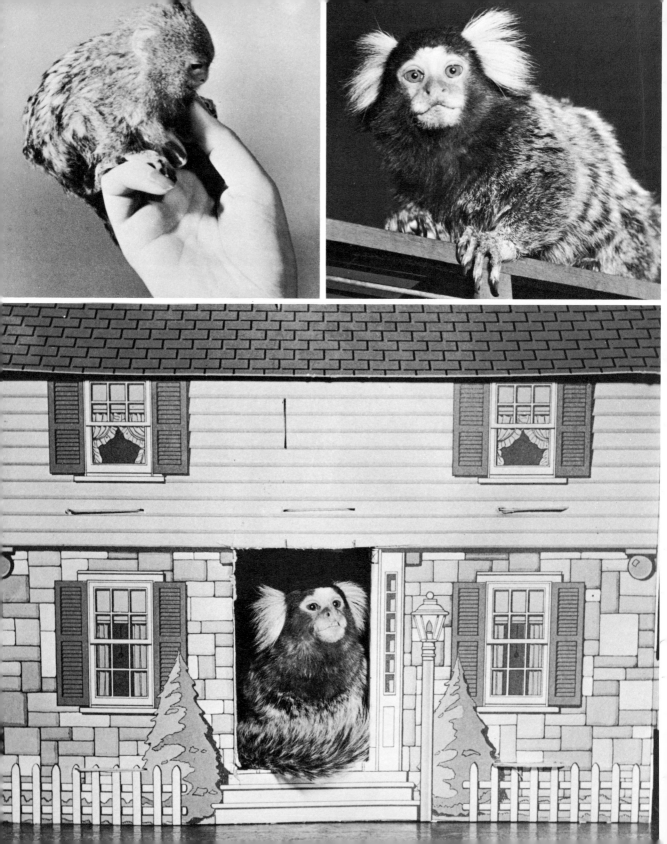

babies to the mother, but as soon as they have finished nursing he takes them back again.

Marmosets have small claws on the digits of both hands and feet, and only the big toes have flat nails. Zoologically they are put into a group by themselves, somewhere between the true monkeys and the prosimians. Many of these tiny primates have become so rare that they are now protected by law.

Marmosets must be kept out of drafts and at a temperature not lower than seventy degrees. They should be kept in pairs (not necessarily of the same species) so that they can play together, groom each other, and huddle together when sleeping. The cage could be a large bird cage or, better still, a cage about forty inches long, thirty inches wide, and forty or fifty inches high. It must contain small branches, a shelf, and a sleeping box or a hollow log. The little animals should be let out of the cage for exercise as often as possible. Because of their small size, marmosets are not as destructive in the home as a larger monkey, but it still best to keep an eye on them. A doll's house is a nice toy for them to scurry in and out of and for playing hide and seek.

Marmosets eat a lot of insects and must be given a variety of mealworms, moths, beetles, grasshoppers, or crickets. (It is possible to buy crickets at pet stores or stores that sell fishing bait.) Fruit for the little primates must be cut into small pieces or diced—even a grape might have to be cut in half. Some marmosets will not eat monkey pellets but like uncooked oatmeal, sunflower seeds, and canned unsweetened fruits. Some prefer milk to water, and fruit juices are usually liked by all. Multiple vitamin drops and cod-liver oil are essential to keep them healthy.

The douroucouli or owl monkey is the only true monkey that is active at night. Like all night creatures it has very large eyes. The white markings around the eyes make it resemble an owl. It comes from the tropical forests of Panama and northern South America. It is very often sold as a pet, since it is fairly docile when young. Older ones usually become high-strung and the needle-sharp teeth can inflict a bad bite. It can spend its days

in a medium-sized cage provided it is let out to play in the evenings. If it does not want to return to its cage, one can easily coax it back with its favorite food: mealworms. Most douroucoulis like to eat hard-boiled eggs, grapes, onions, bananas, and diced, canned, unsweetened fruit. They can be trained to wear a belt around their waists so that they can be taken outdoors for exercise and to catch their own insects.

Among the Old World monkeys sometimes sold in pet shops are the macaques, baboons, and guenons. Few of them are desirable pets, and many are very rough, aggressive, and extremely hard to handle.

Old World monkeys come from Africa and Asia and usually live in large, closely-knit troupes. This gives them protection from their enemies. Some of them, like the baboons and the mandrills, are ground dwellers, although they usually return to the treetops at night to sleep.

In ancient Egypt some baboons were regarded as holy and were reportedly trained to pray, to help the priests, and even to sweep out the temples. But in spite of this claim it would hardly be practical to try to train a baboon to do your household chores.

Baboons have very long muzzles and are sometimes called dog-faced monkeys. They are the largest of the true monkeys. Dominant males are very protective and see to it that no harm comes to a baboon mother or her infant. Even after two years, when the youngster is on its own, the older males act as guardians.

The macaques, to which group the well-known rhesus monkey belongs, are always sold when very young. At that time they are very friendly and playful. They are hardy in captivity and easy to feed and care for, but when they are mature their temperament becomes unreliable.

Hundreds of thousands of these monkeys are imported every year for laboratory research. The term "Rh factor" describes a certain blood type. This blood type was first discovered in rhesus monkeys and named after the first two letters of this monkey's name. In India they are regarded as holy.

All the macaques breed freely in captivity and can be kept outdoors all year round, provided they have a sheltered sleeping place. They eat almost all fruits and vegetables, monkey pellets, cooked rice, and some meat.

Guenons are another group of monkeys that we often find for sale. There are about a hundred varieties of guenons known. Among them are the moustached monkey, the spot-nose monkey, the diana monkey, the DeBrazza's monkey, and the monas, vervets, and talapoins. All guenons have slender bodies, long legs, and long straight tails. They live in small troupes in Africa. Guenons are graceful and active tree dwellers, and they are often very colorful.

Vervet monkey   *Diana monkey*

One of the most beautifully colored guenons is probably the diana monkey. It is mostly black, but the lower part of the body is a rich chestnut-brown, and it has a white goatee, a white throat and chest, and white trim on its ears. On its forehead is a white crest which resembles the symbol of the moon goddess, Diana. These monkeys are friendly and docile when young and do not become as nasty as some other varieties when fully grown. They need a very large cage and lots of sunshine. They are often noisy, touchy, and aloof.

The prosimians, or half-monkeys, as they are sometimes called, are often advertised as monkeys that are easy to keep, need little care, are quiet and gentle, eat everything, and can be kept in a very small space. Nothing could be further from the truth. Although they need much less room than a spider monkey, they are quite delicate and difficult to keep. Some are very lively and some are as large as a house cat. They are called quiet because they are mostly nocturnal and therefore asleep when a prospective customer sees them in the store in the daytime. When they wake up at night, they need space to climb, romp, and jump. Some of the lower primates do not breed in captivity, and the demand for the pet trade has depleted their numbers in their native land severely. Most of them *do* bite, require specialized diets, are prone to sickness, and are not as responsive and intelligent as the true monkeys.

All the true lemurs come from Madagascar and some nearby islands. Almost all of them live in trees and seldom come to

the ground. They have pointed faces, bushy tails, and a long curved nail on the second toe which they use for grooming and scratching. Some lemurs are brown, some black, some have white rings on their tails, some are reddish brown or buff, and several species have ruffs and crests on their heads. Their food habits vary. While some eat mostly insects, others seem to be entirely vegetarian. Most of them are diurnal, which means "active during the daytime," but some of them are nocturnal.

Lemurs breed quite easily in captivity, and the lemur mother is a very patient and devoted parent. Her offspring plays with her by climbing all over her, pulling her fur, and tweaking her nose. Their cage must be roomy, warm, and dry.

The pottos from Africa have thick, plushy fur of different shades, from honey color to grayish brown. They are about sixteen to eighteen inches long and have extremely short tails and very large eyes. The index finger on each hand is a mere stump, and on the foot the second digit terminates in a scratching claw while the other digits have flat nails.

At night the pottos prowl slowly and unhurriedly through the branches, a habit which has earned them the nickname "softly-softly," but they can move quickly when alarmed. The potto has an extension of the neck vertebrae, which can be felt under the skin like blunt, bony points. No one knows for sure what they are for.

Young pottos become very tame in captivity, but adults seldom do. They like to eat bananas, canned diced fruit, and

grapes. They eat insects and can be trained to eat small bits of chopped meat or dog food. Vegetables should be cut into bite-size pieces and sometimes even cooked. Milk and vitamins should also be fed. Pottos should be kept at about seventy-five degrees, and their cage must have branches for climbing and a sleeping shelf as high as possible.

When a potto has the run of the house, it likes to hide and will crawl into odd places. It might crawl into a stove, or hide in a pot or a lady's handbag. Then it puts up quite a fight when one tries to dislodge it. Because it moves so slowly and cautiously, it is not too destructive to objects in the home. The potto can be taught to eat in the daytime, but it is almost impossible to convert him into a day-loving creature.

The lorises are closely related to the pottos, and to the lay-

man they look very similar. They are not often seen for sale. Their native home is in India, Ceylon, and other Oriental regions. They are nocturnal, have large eyes, and some of them have no tail at all. The limbs are usually longer than those of the potto. The housing and care are the same as those of lemurs and pottos.

One tiny primate that is often seen in pet stores is the galago. There are several kinds of galagos, or bush babies. The biggest might be as large as a rabbit; the smallest, the Demidoff's galago, is no bigger than a mouse. They all have long tails, big eyes, and soft fur, usually gray or brown in color. The ears are large and can be folded downwards or backwards.

Bush babies live in tropical Africa, where they jump and leap about in bushes and trees. Their ankles are elongated, and their hands and feet have especially strong grasping power because of disk-like pads. They can easily make leaps of ten feet.

When the smallest of the galagos is young, it can be trained to come to its owner's finger, to jump on his shoulder, or to ride in his shirt pocket. It does not like to be held tightly but enjoys being stroked. Its cage must be large enough so that it can comfortably leap about, and it must be warm and draft-free. Some individuals like to sleep in a box or in a little woollen bag hung in a corner of the cage; others prefer to sleep on a shelf or in an empty birds' nest, which can be set into the fork of a twig.

Bush babies prefer more meat than fruit in their diet. They will eat all kinds of insects, some snails or slugs, and small frogs

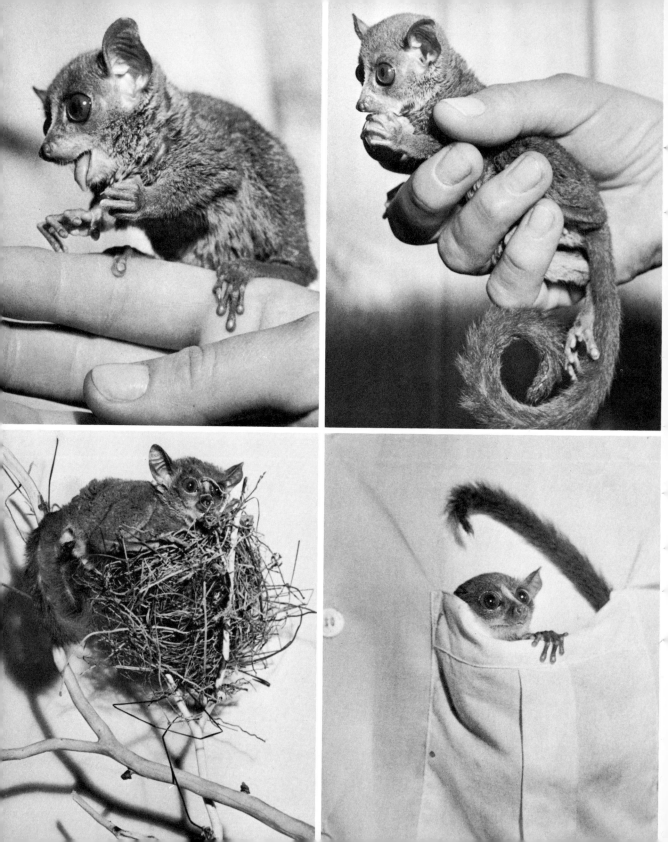

or lizards. The fruit must be cut into small pieces and should be as varied as possible.

The tarsier does not look much like a relative of man, but it too is a primate. Scientists have put it in a class by itself, and it is sometimes called a living fossil because the proportions of its limbs are similar to those of the very early primates. The legs are much longer than the arms, which helps the tarsier greatly when it springs through the trees. The tail is almost naked except for some fine hair on the tip. It is used to balance the animal when it leaps. The eyes are enormous and the ears can be turned backwards, forwards, or sideways. The fingers have flat disks, the nails are triangular and very small, and each foot

has a scratching claw. There are three species, and they all live on the islands ranging from the Philippines to Sumatra. In captivity the tarsiers are delicate, hard to feed, and seldom very tame.

Different from monkeys, and even more fascinating to us, are the four kinds of anthropoid apes, or manlike apes. Apes resemble man closely not only in their anatomy but in their general behavior as well. They have no tails, their arms are longer than their legs, and all can stand and walk erect, although usually just for short periods. The chimpanzee, the orang-utan, and the gorilla use their hands or knuckles as support when they walk on the ground.

The gibbon is the smallest and least manlike of the great apes. It seldom weighs more than twenty pounds, and it stands about eighteen inches to thirty-six inches tall. There are several species and they all come from southeastern Asia and nearby islands. Gibbons are slender, long-armed animals which live mostly in trees. They are extremely graceful and elegant acrobats, swinging, gliding, and jumping high up in the branches. Their genus name is *Hylobates*, which means "tree walkers," and no better description of their way of moving could be given. They can leap thirty feet or more. When they move on the ground, they run erect, with arms raised to balance themselves. In the wild they live in small family units, usually just a male, a female, her new baby, and one or two teen-agers. Early in the morning they vocalize loudly and repeatedly, calling, "whoooop

—whoooop—whoooop." This may be to let other gibbons know
that this family occupies a certain feeding territory and wants
other gibbons to stay out.

Gibbons are afraid to cross water, and many zoos make use
of this aversion by putting the gibbons in a tree-planted enclosure surrounded by a water-filled moat, or by putting them
on a small island in a lake.

In such a natural enclosure gibbons thrive and often breed.
They drink water by standing on the bank of a stream or lake,
or by hanging from branches and dipping their hands into the

water. Then they lick the drops from the fur on the back of their hands. They eat fruits, berries, insects, small birds, and bird eggs.

Unfortunately, they are often sold as pets because the young are very gentle, affectionate, and amusing. But when they mature they often turn unmanageable and can inflict very serious wounds. They may also become aloof and brooding.

Gibbons must have enormously large cages in which to leap and swing about, something the average private person cannot provide. Their health is often delicate and they need lots of sun and the right humidity.

The best-known and best-loved of all the apes are probably the chimpanzees, stars and heros of innumerable movies, television shows, circuses, and books. The reason for their popularity is their high intelligence; their boisterous, outgoing nature; their love of attention and approval; and their friendliness when they are young. But the acts and stunts that these apes are taught to perform do not do them justice. They are dressed in oversized or undersized human clothing and made to play the clown only to show up their shortcomings as compared to man and to strip them of their inborn dignity, self-expression, and intelligence.

Owning a chimp as a pet is something no private person should ever attempt to do, no matter how cute and appealing a baby chimp might be. Since the price is high, six to eight hundred dollars, not many people buy one. Yet the plight

of chimps in pet stores sometimes prompts people to "rescue" them. For a few years a devoted foster parent will enjoy the love, companionship, and dependency of this near-human animal baby. But after a few years the gentle baby becomes a wild adolescent and then a dangerous creature that may weigh close to two hundred pounds.

Since pet chimpanzees form very strong attachments to their owners and become incompatible with their own kind, these animals are not taken by zoos. If they are caged or cruelly chained in some roadside zoo or circus sideshow, they usually perish from grief, lonesomeness, and boredom.

A baby chimp must be cared for like a human baby. It can be bathed; it can be diapered; and it should be dressed when it is cold. It will learn to feed itself with a spoon; it will play with toys or dolls or on a swing; and it gets into mischief just as any toddler might. It should have lots of fresh air and sunshine and regular check-ups by a veterinarian.

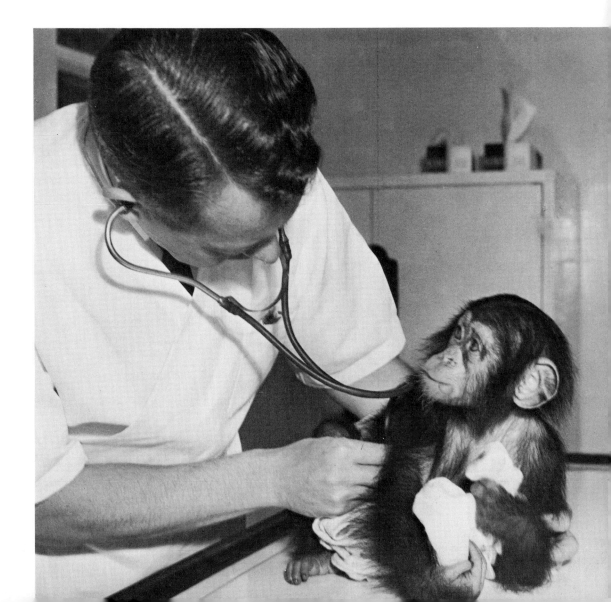

Chimps have many facial expressions that reveal their moods and they learn to respond to and understand many human words. They learn to answer some questions by pointing or other gestures. One pet chimp, for example, seemed to understand over two hundred words. When asked, "Where is the kitten's nose?" she would run off to find the cat, put it on her lap, and point out the nose of the cat. Many scientists have tried to teach chimps to say human words but without great success. Now some attempts are being made to teach them the sign language of the deaf in order to communicate a little better with these animals.

Pet chimps seem to enjoy finger painting and scribbling on paper. "Paintings" made by chimpanzees have been entered in modern art competitions and have even won prizes. But the favorite occupation of young chimps is still climbing, swinging, chasing, and turning somersaults in the woods. They also play with sticks, stones, leaves, and flowers.

In their native Africa chimpanzees live in large troupes. Every night they build sleeping platforms of twigs and leaves high up in trees. Mothers always carry their babies with them and the older children stay close by. Chimps use crude weapons and tools. They use sticks or branches like a club to hit with or to throw at an enemy. They also take thin sticks or long blades of grass and insert them into termite nests or ant hills; then they pull them out and lick off the insects that have crawled onto them.

Many people have tried to train chimps to do menial work in factories or on farms. But a chimp seems to be unable to concentrate and stay with one task longer than ten or fifteen minutes, and no amount of punishment or reward has succeeded in making a slave out of it.

Chimpanzees eat fruits, berries, vegetables, and some meat. In the wild they are known to capture small mammals and even small monkeys. They always munch on leaves at the same time they chew their meat; sometimes they roll the meat into the leaf and eat it like a sandwich. Maybe the leaves help them digest the meat.

The red-haired orang-utan and the black gorilla are so expensive and rare that they are not sold to the public as pets. As babies they are playful and gentle, but when they are grown

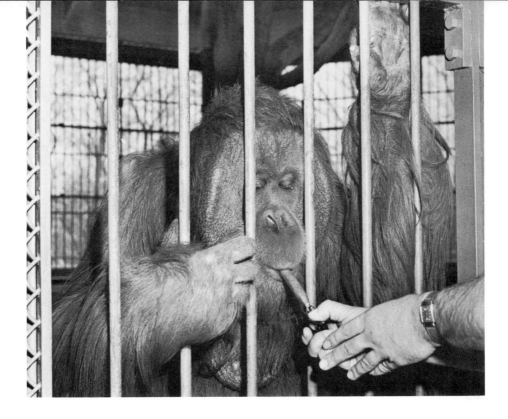

most of them are too powerful to be handled by man. The orang-utan may weight three or four hundred pounds, and a big male gorilla about five or six hundred.

The orang-utan, a name meaning "man of the woods," comes from Borneo and Sumatra and is now in great danger of extinction. Orangs are mainly vegetarians and live a more solitary life than the chimp. When the male orang is fully grown it has enormous fleshy cheek pads.

Young orangs are much more quiet and slower than chimps and can play with one object for a fairly long time before losing interest. When a little orang and a young chimp were each given a mirror to play with, the chimp almost immediately looked behind the mirror to see where the other chimp might be. Failing to find him, the chimp walked away. The little orang, however, kissed and hugged the image for over ten minutes before looking in back of the mirror and finally giving up. It is of course possible that they suddenly realized that they saw their own image.

Gorillas are our largest apes. In the wild, in Africa, they stay mostly on the ground, probably because few trees can support their great weight. At night they build sleeping platforms in sturdy trees. They live in family groups of about ten to twenty individuals and eat mostly leaves, fruits, and roots. The skin of the gorilla is black. Contrary to reports about their ferocious

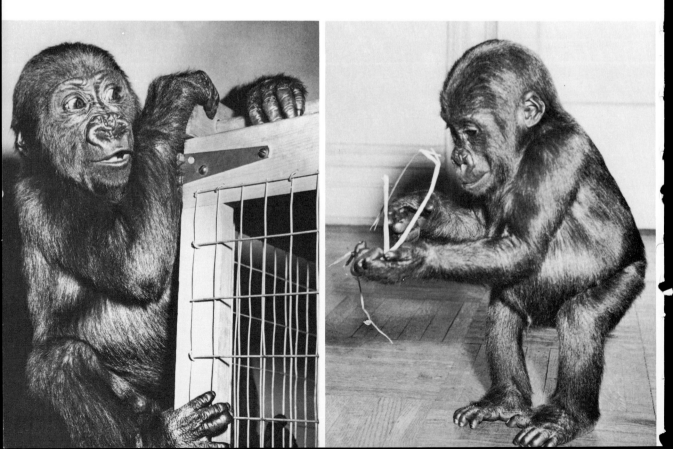

nature, they are shy, peaceful animals. The famous chest beating that an angry male gorilla might do is mostly bluff, and although he rushes angrily toward the enemy, he will stop at a safe distance.

It had been difficult to breed and raise gorillas in captivity until the zoo in Columbus, Ohio, reported the first birth in 1956. Since then several others have been born in different zoos, and others are expected to breed as we learn more about this large primate. Baby gorillas have a gentle, quiet disposition and are sometimes cared for like human infants by zoo personnel if the gorilla mother abandons her child or is unable to care for it.

No matter how interesting and lovable monkeys and apes appear, they should never be kept as house pets. Soon zoos will make greater efforts to exhibit them in more natural settings, with natural things to do, in family groups, or with companionship of their own kind. Only then can we all observe our closest relatives the way they really are—not as unhappy displaced creatures in a bare prison.

A listing of monkeys and apes discussed